STILL PUMPED FROM USING THE MOUSE

A DILBERT® Book by Scott Adams

Andrews and McMeel
A Universal Press Syndicate Company
Kansas City

ATTENTION: SCHOOLS AND BUSINESSES

Andrews and McMeel books are available at quantity discounts with bulk purchase for educational, business, or sales promotional use. For information, write to: Special Sales Department, Andrews and McMeel, 4900 Main Street, Kansas City, Missouri 64112.

I didn't forget this time, Pam.

Other Dilbert Books from Andrews and McMeel

It's Obvious You Won't Survive By Your Wits Alone
ISBN: 0-8362-0415-8

Bring Me the Head of Willy the Mailboy
ISBN: 0-8362-1779-9

Shave the Whales
ISBN: 0-8362-1740-3

Dogbert's Clues for the Clueless
ISBN: 0-8362-1737-3

Build a Better Life by Stealing Office Supplies
ISBN: 0-8362-1757-8

Always Postpone Meetings with Time-Wasting Morons
ISBN: 0-8362-1758-6

For ordering information, call 1-800-642-6480

Introduction

In the past few years several great cartoonists have decided to retire, much to the sadness of their fans. It makes me feel like the guy who took the home movies of the Kennedy assassination—the right side of my brain is saying, "What a horrible tragedy," while the left side is making those little cash register noises.

When the announcement of Bill Watterson's retirement came out several reporters called me to get my reaction. The phone conversations went like this:

Reporter: "What do you think about Watterson retiring?"

Me: "Hee hee. Oops."

Reporter: "Are you giggling?"

Me: "Um, no, I'm weeping over the loss of an excellent comic strip."

Reporter: "What's that music in the background?"

Me: "My cats are forming a conga line. They don't seem to appreciate the sadness of this situation."

Cats: "Tequila!!!!"

Maybe it didn't go exactly like that, but you get the general picture.

Anyway, the question I'm most often asked lately is whether I'm also "burned out" and planning to retire. The answer is no, I haven't made enough money to be "burned out" yet. I only have enough money to feel "tired" or maybe "overworked." And frankly, I blame you readers for that.

In any event, quitting just isn't my style. I'm more likely to hire illegal immigrants to do the writing and drawing for me. They might not bring the same wit and artistic integrity to the strip that I do … and it might not be in English … but let's face it, my work isn't a home run every single day either. It'll probably take a decade for anybody to notice. And by then maybe I'll be "burned out" too.

Speaking of home runs, you can still join Dogbert's New Ruling Class (DNRC) before Dogbert conquers the world and makes everybody else our domestic servants. As you might have noticed, the members of the DNRC are brighter and more attractive than the "induhviduals" who have not joined, so don't be an induhvidual.

To join the DNRC, simply put your name on the list for the free Dilbert Newsletter, published approximately "whenever I feel like it," or about four times a year.

If you want to receive the DNRC Newsletter via e-mail, send your e-mail address to:

ScottAdams@aol.com

If you prefer hard copies of the DNRC Newsletter, via snail mail, send your address to:

Dilbert Mailing List
c/o United Media
200 Madison Avenue
New York, NY 10016

S. Adams

http://www.unitedmedia.com/comics/dilbert/

Panel 1: DILBERT, YOU'RE BEING TEMPORARILY TRANSFERRED TO THE FIELD SALES ORGANIZATION.

Panel 2: NORMALLY WE USE THESE ASSIGNMENTS TO ROUND SOMEBODY OUT FOR MANAGEMENT. BUT IN THIS CASE I'M JUST YANKING YOUR CHAIN!

12-14

Panel 3: YOU'RE OVER-COMMUNICATING AGAIN, SIR.

PLUS, I HATE THE MANAGER OF SALES.

Panel 4: SO... DILBERT, WELCOME TO THE SALES DEPARTMENT. I'M TINA, YOUR NEW BOSS.

HI

Panel 5: AS THE NEW GUY, YOU GET THE CUSTOMERS WHO DESPISE OUR PRODUCTS AND WANT TO HURT US PERSONALLY.

12-15

Panel 6: I HATE YOU! I HATE YOU!

YOU'LL BE SELLING TO THE SMALL BUSINESS MARKET. HE'S YOUR BEST ACCOUNT.

Panel 7: WELCOME TO SALES TRAINING.

Panel 8: AS YOU KNOW, OUR COMPANY MAKES OVER-PRICED, INFERIOR PRODUCTS. WE TRY TO COMPENSATE BY SETTING HIGH SALES QUOTAS.

12-16

Panel 9: WE DON'T ASK YOU TO ACT ILLEGALLY, BUT IT'S PRETTY MUCH THE ONLY WAY TO REACH QUOTA. OKAY, THAT'S IT FOR TRAINING. ANY QUESTIONS?

DILBERT THE SALESMAN...

YOUR COMPETITOR WAS HERE AN HOUR AGO...

HE PROMISED ME A MASSAGE FROM HELGA IF I BUY FROM HIS COMPANY. WHAT'S YOUR OFFER?

I'LL GIVE YOU MY HOUSE FOR HELGA.

YOU'RE NEW AT THIS...

YOU'VE NEVER ACCEPTED ME IN YOUR FAMILY BECAUSE I'M A LITTLE RAT.

BUT I'LL BE TESTING A DRUG AT THE LAB THAT WILL CHANGE THAT. NO MORE LITTLE RAT.

YOU WON'T BE A RAT?

DON'T TELL ME IT'S THE "RAT" PART THAT BOTHERS YOU...

I'M TESTING A GROWTH FORMULA AT THE LAB.

NEWS

I'M SO HAPPY. I'VE OFTEN THOUGHT THAT THE ONLY THING BETTER THAN A RAT IN THE HOUSE IS A <u>GIANT</u> RAT IN THE HOUSE.

NEWS

YESTERDAY I WOULD HAVE BEEN MIFFED AT YOUR SARCASM. BUT THAT WOULDN'T BE "BIG" OF ME.

BETTER YET, A GIANT, <u>WITTY</u> RAT.

GOOD REPORT, BUT CHANGE THE WORD "USE" TO "UTILIZE" IN EACH CASE.

CHANGE "HELP" TO "FACILITATE" AND REPLACE "DO" WITH "IMPLEMENTATION PHASE."

HMM... IT'S STILL A BIT TOO READABLE.

I COULD REDUCE THE TYPE SIZE AND RUN IT THROUGH THE FAX.

NORMALLY I'M ALL STRESSED OUT DURING THE HOLIDAYS, BUT NOT THIS YEAR.

I ELIMINATED MY SHOPPING STRESS BY GETTING EVERYBODY THE "FLABMASTER THIGH-TONING SUPPORT SOCKS".

THEIR COMMERCIALS SOUND BETTER THE CLOSER YOU GET TO CHRISTMAS.

YOU CAN BUILD MUSCLE JUST LYING ON THE COUCH!

I'M COLLECTING MONEY FOR A GIFT TO A POOR FAMILY THIS CHRISTMAS.

WHAT ARE YOU BUYING FOR THEM?

A CD PLAYER.

THANK YOU FOR MAKING THIS THE MOST SHALLOW GESTURE OF MY LIFE.

I'LL ADD YOUR NAME TO THE CARD.

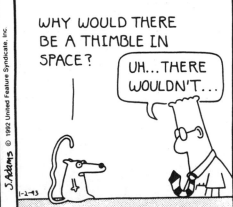

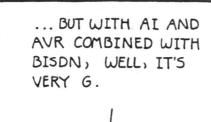

"ALTHOUGH RAISING CHILDREN IS DIFFICULT, BE ASSURED THAT YOU WILL GET HELP FROM A POWER GREATER THAN YOURSELF."

"TEACH YOUR CHILDREN ABOUT THE HIGHER POWER AND ABOUT THE 'GREAT BOOK' WHICH WILL GIVE THEM DIRECTION."

THEY'RE CALLED "TV LISTINGS." WITHOUT THEM, YOU'RE JUST FLIPPING.

THERE'S DILBERT... I'LL SNEAK UP AND HUG HIS LEG UNTIL HE LOVES ME AND ACCEPTS ME IN THE FAMILY.

© 1993 United Feature Syndicate, Inc.

A RAT IS CLINGING TO MY LEG.

I HAD THAT PROBLEM TILL I SWITCHED TO "OLD SPICE."

MY NEW STYLE OF MANAGEMENT IS EXHAUSTING ME.

I HEARD SOME PEOPLE TALKING ABOUT "MBWA" OR "MANAGEMENT BY WALKING AROUND."

I WALKED ALL THE WAY TO THE PARK AND BACK. BUT I CAN'T SAY THAT I SEE MUCH IMPROVEMENT AROUND HERE.

I'M FEELING ILL. I THINK I'LL STAY HOME TODAY.

GREAT... NOW YOU'LL TRY TO MAKE ME FEEL SORRY FOR YOU SO I'LL WAIT ON YOU ALL DAY WELL, THAT'S A LOUSY THING TO DO TO A FRIEND.

GEE, I'M SORRY. CAN I GET YOU ANYTHING WHILE I'M UP?

TEA WITH LEMON. AND SOME WAFFLES.

TO PROTECT OUR ENVIRONMENT, I'VE ORDERED THAT INK BE REMOVED FROM ALL COPIERS, PRINTERS AND PENS.

RESEARCH SHOWS THAT MANY SQUIDS CAN BE SPARED BY REDUCING OUR INK USAGE.

I DON'T THINK WE GET OUR INK FROM SQUIDS, SIR.

OH, RIGHT... NEXT YOU'LL SAY WE DON'T GET OUR "ELMER'S" GLUE FROM COWS.

FIRST ON THE AGENDA IS A DISCUSSION OF THE COMANY'S NEW PAPER RECYCLING PROGRAM.

WE TALKED ABOUT THAT LAST TIME... HEY, THIS IS LAST WEEK'S AGENDA.

YOU SPOTTED THE ONE DRAWBACK.

22

SOMETIMES I WONDER, HOW WOULD MY LIFE BE DIFFERENT IF ALL WHALES WERE EXTINCT?

IT'S NOT LIKE THEY DO ANYTHING FOR US. YOU NEVER HEAR OF SEEING-EYE WHALES. THEY CAN'T FETCH THE PAPER OR DRAG YOU OUT OF A BURNING BUILDING...

DON'T YOU THINK THE WORLD HAS TOO MANY FAT, WORTHLESS, MAMMALS?

I WAS JUST THINKING THAT, SIR.

HERE'S MY NEW BUSINESS CARD. I'M A ROMANCE INTERPRETER.

FOR A SMALL FEE I'LL ACCOMPANY YOU ON DATES AND TRANSLATE BETWEEN MALE AND FEMALE LANGUAGE.

SHE'S TELLING A POINTLESS STORY ABOUT WORK. BY ANNOYING YOU IN THIS WAY SHE HOPES TO FORM A CLOSER BOND.

BLAH BLAH BLAH

DOGBERT IS A ROMANCE INTERPRETER

HE'S TELLING YOU HOW TO LOGICALLY SOLVE ALL OF THE EMOTIONAL PROBLEMS YOU SEEM TO HAVE.

BLAH BLAH BLAH

HE REASONS THAT IF HE CAN FIX YOUR PROBLEMS HE WON'T HAVE TO HEAR ABOUT THEM ANYMORE.

BLAH BLAH BLAH

HE HOPES THAT THE WISDOM AND COMPASSION HE JUST FAKED WAS ENOUGH TO AROUSE YOU. NOW HE WILL TALK ABOUT HIMSELF.

BLAH BLAH ME

25

PETER, YOU'RE A BRILLIANT COMPUTER PROGRAMMER AND YOU LIKE YOUR JOB.

ALTHOUGH YOU LACK ANY SOCIAL AWARENESS AND CANNOT COMMUNICATE WITH YOUR SPECIES, I DECIDED TO PROMOTE YOU TO MANAGEMENT.

DON'T BE AFRAID... IT'S CALLED A NECKTIE.

YESTERDAY I WAS A COMPUTER PROGRAMMER AND TODAY I'M YOUR NEW SUPERVISOR.

THE HARDEST PART IS MASTERING THESE DANG MANAGEMENT CLOTHES. DID YOU KNOW THEY DON'T COME WITH AN INSTRUCTION MANUAL?

I'LL HAVE TO CALL THEIR "800" HELP LINE AGAIN.

WHERE ARE WE NOW?

I CAN'T TELL YOU. THAT'S PART OF THE EXPERIMENT.

I READ IN "READER'S DIGEST" HOW A DOG FOUND HIS WAY HOME FROM A HUNDRED MILES AWAY. I WANT TO TEST YOUR HOMING INSTINCT.

OKAY, I THINK WE'RE READY TO BEGIN...

THE COMPANY IS A BILLION DOLLARS BELOW ITS EARNINGS PROJECTIONS.

FROM NOW ON, ONLY THE MANAGERS AT MY LEVEL OR ABOVE MAY EAT DONUTS AT COMPANY MEETINGS.

THIS WON'T BE EASY FOR ANY OF US. HECK, I DON'T EVEN KNOW IF I CAN EAT THIS MANY DONUTS.

THEIR CARS ARE ALWAYS CLEAN

THEY WRITE LETTERS TO EXPRESS THEIR OUTRAGE

Dear Editor,
The funny pages is no place for sarcasm! Think about the children!

THEY READ THE SAME BOOK MORE THAN ONCE.

THEY ARE THE PEOPLE WITH WAY TOO MUCH TIME ON THEIR HANDS.

HEE HEE

HI, GUYS. I'M WENDELL J. STONE THE FOURTH, RECENT STANFORD MBA AND BRAND NEW TO THE WORKFORCE.

LOOK, "WEN-DULL," WE AREN'T IMPRESSED BY YOUR EDUCATION. AT THIS COMPANY IT'S THE QUALITY OF YOUR WORK THAT COUNTS!

I'M YOUR NEW SENIOR VICE PRESIDENT, AND I WANT YOU TO LICK THE TAR OFF MY PORSCHE NOW.

OKAY, BUT WATCH THE QUALITY OF MY WORK!

DOGBERT IS A CREATIVITY CONSULTANT

WE DON'T NEED ANY OF YOUR "INTUITION" MUMBO JUMBO. WE NEED QUANTITATIVE DATA!

THE ONLY WAY TO MAKE DECISIONS IS TO PULL NUMBERS OUT OF THE AIR, CALL THEM "ASSUMPTIONS," AND CALCULATE THE NET PRESENT VALUE.

OF COURSE, YOU HAVE TO USE THE RIGHT DISCOUNT RATE, OTHERWISE IT'S MEANINGLESS.

GO AWAY.

DOGBERT IS A CREATIVITY CONSULTANT

HERE'S MY FINAL REPORT ON YOUR COMPANY.

I'VE CONCLUDED THAT YOU'RE DOOMED. YOU WASTE TOO MUCH MONEY ON CONSULTANTS.

YOU'RE A CONSULTANT.

IRONIC, ISN'T IT?

THIS IS IT... THE CRITICAL THIRD DATE.

THIS IS WHEN THEY CASUALLY MENTION ANY HIDDEN DEFORMITIES OR HORRIBLE SECRETS TO SEE IF YOU STILL LIKE THEM.

SOME PEOPLE SAY YOU SHOULD STOP DATING AFTER YOU MARRY A MOB BOSS.

IN ORDER TO BUILD TEAM SPIRIT I'VE DECIDED YOU SHOULD HAVE LUNCH TOGETHER ONCE A WEEK.

I WON'T BE THERE MYSELF BECAUSE IT WOULD SERIOUSLY CUT INTO MY FREE TIME.

BESIDES, IT'S MY JOB TO MOTIVATE, NOT GET BOGGED DOWN IN THE DETAILS.

WHAT ARE YOU UP TO, TED?

I'M WORKING LIKE A DOG LATELY.

I'D BETTER NOT ASK.

SCRATCH SCRATCH

I FOUND A TYPO IN THE BUDGET SPREAD-SHEET... IT'S TOO LATE TO FIX IT.

WE TRANSFERRED ONE JOB TO ANOTHER GROUP BUT ACCIDENTALLY KEPT THE MONEY AND HEAD-COUNT.

...SO, WE STILL PAY YOU BUT YOU AREN'T ALLOWED TO DO WORK.

THIS IS THE HAPPIEST DAY OF MY LIFE.

I'VE GOT GOOD NEWS AND BAD NEWS.

THE BAD NEWS IS THAT HUGE COMPANIES LIKE US CAN'T COMPETE AGAINST SMALL, NIMBLE COMPANIES. THE GOOD NEWS IS THAT AT THIS RATE _WE'LL_ BE THE SMALLEST COMPANY AROUND.

WHAT AM I DOING WRONG HERE?

WE'RE NUMBER ONE!

WE'RE NUMBER ONE!

YES!!

HEY, WALLY, HOW DID YOU GET A ROOF FOR YOUR CUBICLE?

THIS STUFF IS ALL MODULAR. YOU JUST TAKE SOME IDIOT'S WALL AND MAKE IT YOUR CEILING.

BY ANY CHANCE, DO YOU KNOW WHAT HAPPENED TO _MY_ WALL?

WHAT DID IT LOOK LIKE?

DO YOU NOTICE ANYTHING DIFFERENT?

NO.

I'M WEARING CONTACT LENSES.

THEN WHY ARE YOU STILL WEARING GLASSES?

THEY'RE MY EMERGENCY BACKUP SYSTEM.

YOUR PANTS ARE ON BACKWARDS.

I'M WRITING A BOOK ABOUT BEING TRAPPED IN THE SPACE HOLE FOR THREE HUNDRED THOUSAND YEARS.

Day One: I thought about cheese. Day two: See Day One. Day three: See Day One two...

DO YOU KNOW A GOOD EDITOR?

WE'RE HAVING A DEPARTMENT BOWLING NIGHT TOMORROW.

IT'S MY WAY OF REWARDING ALL OF YOU FOR YOUR PERFORMANCE THIS QUARTER.

WE HATE DOING THINGS TOGETHER AT NIGHT.

I WASN'T HAPPY WITH YOUR PERFORMANCE.

WOULD YOU LIKE TO POSE FOR MY NEW CALENDAR, "THE MEN OF ENGINEERING"?

I HOPE TO DISPEL THE MYTH THAT ENGINEERS ARE OUT OF SHAPE AND UNAWARE OF WHAT OTHERS ARE THINKING.

I'M STILL KIND OF "PUMPED" FROM USING THE MOUSE.

TAKE OFF YOUR SHIRT.

HI, I'M TIM ZUMPH, WRITER OF THE FAMOUS MEMO OF FEBRUARY THIRD, 1978...

I REMEMBER IT SO CLEARLY. MY BOSS WALKED RIGHT UP AND SAID "NICE MEMO, TIM." AND IT WASN'T EVEN TIME FOR MY ANNUAL PERFORMANCE REVIEW.

I STILL KEEP A COPY WITH ME.

TYPO...

FROM NOW ON, YOUR RAISES WILL BE PARTLY DEPENDENT ON AN EVALUATION BY YOUR CO-WORKERS.

HYPOTHETICALLY, IF MY CO-WORKERS GOT SMALL RAISES THEN WOULDN'T THERE BE MORE AVAILABLE IN THE BUDGET FOR ME?

THAT DIDN'T LAST LONG, EVEN BY OUR STANDARDS.

I'VE BEEN SAYING FOR YEARS THAT "EMPLOYEES ARE OUR MOST VALUABLE ASSET."

IT TURNS OUT THAT I WAS WRONG. MONEY IS OUR MOST VALUABLE ASSET. EMPLOYEES ARE NINTH.

I'M AFRAID TO ASK WHAT CAME IN EIGHTH.

CARBON PAPER.

LOOK EVERYONE, I'M ENGAGED!

HEY, IT'S ONE OF THOSE "NEAR DIAMOND" RINGS THEY WERE SELLING ON THE TV SHOPPING CHANNEL FOR $29.95.

UH... OF COURSE IT HAS A LIST PRICE OF OVER A HUNDRED DOLLARS...

OOH, GOOD SAVE.

GEE, LINDA, IF YOU DON'T MIND SOME CONSTRUCTIVE CRITICISM, THAT DRESS MAKES YOU LOOK PUDGY.

HAAIII!!!

I STILL DON'T UNDERSTAND WOMEN, BUT I THINK WHEN THEY YELL "HAAIII" IT MEANS THEY LIKE THE DRESS THEY'RE WEARING.

I DON'T UNDERSTAND WHY PHOTOGRAPHERS TRY SO HARD TO GET EMBARRASSING PICTURES OF CELEBRITIES.

HECK, I COULD JUST SCAN THE CELEBRITY PHOTOS INTO MY COMPUTER AND CREATE ANY EMBARRASSING SITUATION YOU CAN THINK OF.

I THINK CINDY CRAWFORD SHOULD LOOK MORE REPULSED.

THIS IS BEFORE WE KISS.

Panel 1: I JUST READ THAT A NEW COMPUTER CHIP IS ON THE MARKET. YOUR MACHINE IS OUT OF DATE.

Panel 2: YOU'RE BEHIND THE CURVE. TECHNOLOGY IS RACING AHEAD WITHOUT YOU. YOU'RE NO LONGER STATE-OF-THE-ART OR LEADING EDGE.

Panel 3: SOMETIMES PEOPLE LIKE YOU CAN GET JOBS IN MUSEUMS.

I BOUGHT THIS THING YESTERDAY!!

Panel 4: I'M SO MAD... I JUST BOUGHT A NEW COMPUTER AND IT'S ALREADY OBSOLETE.

Panel 5: DON'T FEEL BAD. THE OTHER ENGINEERS WON'T LOOK DOWN ON YOU JUST BECAUSE YOU'RE BEHIND THE TECHNOLOGY CURVE.

Panel 6: YEAH, WE WILL.

NOT RIGHT IN FRONT OF HIM.

Panel 7: LAPTOP COMPUTERS ARE OUTDATED. YOU WANT OUR NEW FINGERNAIL MODELS.

SALE 50¢

NEW ↓

Panel 8: YOU GLUE THEM PERMANENTLY TO EACH NAIL. THEY SENSE WHERE EACH FINGER IS AT ALL TIMES. YOU DON'T NEED A KEYBOARD.

Panel 9: OF COURSE, SOME PEOPLE PREFER THAT THEIR COMPUTER NOT KNOW WHERE THEIR FINGERS ARE AT ALL TIMES.

DAVE, ABOUT LAST NIGHT...

I'M GOING TO START A BUSINESS AS A PROFESSIONAL INSULTER.

FOR EXAMPLE, I WOULD SAY TO YOU, YOU'RE SO UGLY YOU HAVE TO WEAR A DISGUISE ON GARBAGE PICK-UP DAY.

THAT WAS UNCALLED FOR.

WELL, THEN NO CHARGE.

YES?

I HAVE A DOGBERT INSULT-O-GRAM FROM YOUR EX-WIFE...

YOU'RE SO UGLY, WEATHER SATELLITES WON'T PHOTOGRAPH YOUR TOWN UNLESS IT'S CLOUDY.

THE SMARTER PEOPLE RECOGNIZE THIS AS A TIPPING SITUATION.

I'M NOT LOOKING FOR ROMANCE. NO, I JUST WANT TO BE FRIENDS.

THAT'S ALL? BUT WHY??

BECAUSE YOU HAVE A SNOUT LIKE A PORPOISE.

WHEN YOU USE REVERSE PSYCHOLOGY, IT'S BEST TO LEAVE OUT UNFLATTERING REFERENCES TO OTHER MAMMALS.

DILBERT, I NEED YOU TO STOP EVERYTHING AND DO THIS EMERGENCY BUDGET EXERCISE.

ESTIMATE THE BUDGET IMPACT OF REPLACING ALL THE ENGINEERS WITH DECORATIVE PLANTS.

LATER, I'LL SUMMARIZE EVERYBODY'S INPUTS INTO A BULLET POINT, LIKE "OXYGEN IS GOOD."

WOULD THESE BE RENTED PLANTS?

I SUMMARIZED THE BUDGET IMPACTS ON SIX HUNDRED PROJECTS WITH THOSE THREE BULLET POINTS.

"– OXYGEN IS GOOD
– COMPETITION IS BAD
– I LIKE JELLO"

DO YOU THINK IT'S TOO DETAILED FOR THE SENIOR EXECUTIVES?

TAKE OUT THE "COMPETITION" ONE.

I THINK I'M EVOLVING INTO A FLYING RAT.

I NOTICED THAT MY ARMS ARE FLATTER THAN MY PARENTS' ARMS. IN A MILLION YEARS THIS NATURAL ADVANTAGE WILL BECOME WINGS!

THERE GOES THE HAPPIEST RAT I KNOW.

TOO SOON.

EVOLUTION TAKES MILLIONS OF YEARS, RATBERT. YOU'LL BE LONG GONE BEFORE RATS DEVELOP FLYING SKILLS.

THAT'S WHAT THEY SAID TO THE WRIGHT BROTHERS.

BUT THEY BUILT AN AIRPLANE.

DON'T YOU THINK THEY TRIED THIS FIRST?

FLAP FLAP FLAP FLAP

DILBERT SAYS IT'S IMPOSSIBLE TO FLY BY FLAPPING YOUR ARMS. IS HE RIGHT, BOB?

IT JUST DEPENDS HOW HARD YOU FLAP.

IT MUST BE EMBARRASSING TO BE YOU.

NEWS

THAT'S $1.89

JUST FOR SIMPLICITY, I'LL GIVE YOU $7.14

AS AN ENGINEER, I FEEL A PROFESSIONAL RESPONSIBILITY TO MAKE THINGS EASY FOR PEOPLE.

...CARRY THE THREE.

IF I DON'T GET SOME LOVE AND SUPPORT AROUND HERE, I MIGHT TURN TO A LIFE OF HEINOUS CRIME...

OR WORSE, I COULD BECOME A CERTIFIED PUBLIC ACCOUNTANT...

STOP IT. YOU'RE SCARING ME...

I'M GOOD WITH NUMBERS.

I HAVE TO GIVE A SPEECH TO THE "SOCIETY OF ENGINEERS" TODAY... I'M A BIT NERVOUS.

SOMETIMES YOU CAN RELAX BY IMAGINING THE AUDIENCE IS NAKED.

WHOA! CANCEL THAT. I JUST PICTURED FOUR HUNDRED NAKED ENGINEERS.

TOO LATE.

... AS YOU APPROACHED THE SPEED OF LIGHT YOU WOULD BECOME INFINITELY DENSE.

THEN WOULD YOU BE FORCED TO TAKE A JOB AS A HIGH SCHOOL GYM TEACHER?

THE BOOK CHANGES SUBJECTS AT THIS POINT.

SOUNDS LIKE A COVER-UP.

A SMALL BAND OF THE CREATURES WERE KNOWN TO LIVE HIGH IN AN ARTIFICIAL STRUCTURE.

ON MY WAY TO STUDY THEM I TOOK NOTE OF THE NATIVE VEGETATION.

RENTED

THE YOUNGER MALES WERE AT PLAY. THEY BECAME SELF-CONSCIOUS WHEN WATCHED.

THE DOMINANT MALE HAD A GRAY BACK. HE CONTROLLED THE OTHERS BY WAVING LITTLE ENVELOPES.

THERE WERE FEW FEMALES IN THE GROUP. THE LESS DOMINANT MALES HAD NO CHANCE OF MATING.

UNLIKE OTHER SPECIES THEY HAD NO INSTINCT FOR GROOMING.

WANT TO GROOM?

DROP DEAD.

4-11

MY TIME WAS UP. BUT I WILL MISS THEM, THOSE...

ENGINEERS IN THE MIST

HOW LONG ARE YOU SUPPOSED TO MICROWAVE POPCORN?

57

DON'T GET TOO CLOSE-- I FOUND OUT THAT MY BALDNESS IS CAUSED BY TOO MUCH TESTOSTERONE.

NOW WITH MY HAIR GONE I'M AFRAID THE TESTOSTERONE WILL START FLINGING OUT OF MY PORES.

4-12

HEY! YOU GOT SOME ON MY SHIRT!

DO YOU HAVE A PROBLEM WITH THAT?

BEING BALD ISN'T SO BAD. WITH ALL THIS TESTOSTERONE, MEN WILL FEAR ME AND WOMEN WILL DESIRE ME.

4-13

TAKE A HIKE, FUZZY. SHE'S MINE NOW.

I DO FIND YOU STRANGELY ATTRACTIVE.

TESTOSTERONE; YOU'RE HELPLESS.

GEE, WALLY, YOU SURE HAVE BEEN POPULAR WITH WOMEN SINCE THE TESTOSTERONE STARTED SPEWING FROM YOUR HEAD.

4-14

IT'S AMAZING... I EVEN BOUGHT A PICKUP TRUCK AND A RIFLE SO I CAN HUNT AFTER WORK.

WHAT DO YOU HUNT AROUND HERE?

PIGEONS ARE THE MOST CONVENIENT... DON'T EVEN HAVE TO GET OUT OF THE TRUCK.

S. Adams © 1993 United Feature Syndicate, Inc.

58

MAYBE IT'S BECAUSE OF MY HIGH TESTOSTERONE LEVELS, BUT I COULDN'T RESIST GETTING MY PICKUP JACKED UP.

I THOUGHT IT WOULD BE MORE FRIGHTENING TO THE PEOPLE I TAILGATE.

THE ONLY PROBLEM IS THAT YOU CAN'T LET PEOPLE SEE YOU TRYING TO GET IN IT.

LIFE HAS BEEN GREAT SINCE THE TESTOSTERONE STARTED SPEWING FROM MY HEAD.

IT LOOKS LIKE THE FLOW IS STOPPING.

WAIT-A-MINUTE. WHY WAS I TOUCHING YOU?

I HOPE YOU WON'T BE SHALLOW ABOUT THIS.

...AND PEOPLE WHO DON'T BOTHER TO VOTE HAVE NO RIGHT TO COMPLAIN.

WHY NOT?

WHY NOT? IT'S OBVIOUS. NO VOTE MEANS NO RIGHT TO COMPLAIN. YOU CAN'T GET MUCH MORE LOGICAL THAN THAT.

BESIDES, THAT'S HOW I WAS RAISED.

YOU WERE RAISED BY BUMPER STICKERS?

THE LOCAL SCHOOL WANTS SOMEBODY TO TALK TO THE KIDS ABOUT A CAREER AS AN ENGINEER.

I'M GIVING THIS PLUM ASSIGNMENT TO YOU BECAUSE YOU'RE SUCH A GOOD ROLE MODEL.

HEE HEE

IT'S MORE SINCERE SOUNDING WHEN YOU DON'T GIGGLE.

REMEMBER, CHILDREN ARE OUR FUTURE!

DILBERT HAS AGREED TO TALK TO THE CLASS ABOUT EXCITING CAREERS IN THE FIELD OF ENGINEERING!

THERE'S MORE TO BEING AN ENGINEER THAN JUST WRITING TECHNICAL MEMOS THAT NOBODY READS.

ONCE IN A WHILE, SOMEBODY READS ONE. THEN YOU HAVE TO FIND A SCAPEGOAT, OR USE SOME VACATION TIME AND HOPE IT ALL BLOWS OVER.

DILBERT TALKS TO A CLASS ABOUT CAREER OPTIONS.

ENGINEERING IS ONE OF THE BEST CAREERS AVAILABLE.

FOR THE NEXT TWENTY YEARS I'LL SIT IN A BIG BOX CALLED A CUBICLE. IT'S LIKE A RESTROOM STALL BUT WITH LOWER WALLS.

I SPEND MOST OF MY TIME HOPING THE ELECTROMAGNETIC FIELDS FROM MY OFFICE EQUIPMENT AREN'T KILLING ME.

DILBERT TALKS TO A CLASS ABOUT CAREER OPTIONS.

AND DON'T FORGET THE SOCIAL LIFE THAT COMES WITH BEING AN ENGINEER.

NINETY PERCENT OF ALL ENGINEERS ARE GUYS, SO IT'S A BONANZA OF DATING OPPORTUNITIES FOR THE LADIES WHO ENTER THE FIELD.

FOR THE MEN, THERE ARE THESE LITTLE VIDEO GAME DEVICES...

BEEP BEEP

WOULD I BE ALLOWED TO DATE A NON-ENGINEER?

DILBERT TALKS TO A CLASS ABOUT CAREER OPTIONS.

THE GOAL OF EVERY ENGINEER IS TO RETIRE WITHOUT GETTING BLAMED FOR A MAJOR CATASTROPHE.

ENGINEERS PREFER TO WORK AS "CONSULTANTS" ON PROJECT TEAMS. THAT WAY THERE'S NO REAL WORK, BLAME IS SPREAD ACROSS THE GROUP, AND YOU CAN CRUSH ANY IDEA FROM MARKETING!

...AND SOMETIMES YOU GET FREE DONUTS JUST FOR SHOWING UP!

GET OUT OF MY CLASS-ROOM.

LOOK WHAT I GOT FOR MY COMPUTER! IT'S A ROMOSTATIC REAL-TIME DATA COMPRESSION PROCESSOR!

OOOH... I CAN'T WAIT TO PLUG YOU IN, MY LITTLE DARLING. I'VE WAITED SO LONG.

OH YES! YES!

DOES THE CHURCH KNOW ABOUT THIS?

62

Panel 1: I'M GOING TO START-UP A TELEVISION NEWS NETWORK THAT ONLY REPORTS HAPPY STORIES.

Panel 2: IN SPORTS, FIFTY PERCENT OF THE TEAMS WON THEIR GAMES YESTERDAY. AND ALL THE PLAYERS ARE MILLIONAIRES — MOST OF WHOM HAVE NO SERIOUS DRUG PROBLEMS.

Panel 3: OUR PERSON OF THE WEEK IS DARRYL, WHO, DESPITE HIS TINY BRAIN, FOUND SUCCESS THROUGH A LIFE OF CRIME.

Panel 4: DOGBERT'S GOOD NEWS SHOW

NINE OUT OF TEN PEOPLE HAVE JOBS... THREE BILLION PEOPLE HAD A NICE DAY TODAY... AND THE FOREST HAS PLENTY OF OWLS.

Panel 5: REGULAR NEWS SHOW

A HUGE ASTEROID COULD DESTROY EARTH! AND BY COINCIDENCE, THAT'S THE SUBJECT OF TONIGHT'S MINISERIES.

WE'LL ALL DIE!!

Panel 6: BACK TO DOGBERT...

IN SCIENCE, RESEARCHERS PROVED THAT THIS SIMPLE DEVICE CAN KEEP IDIOTS OFF OF YOUR TELEVISION SCREEN.

CLICK

Panel 7: ...THEN I SAID "WHAT ABOUT AN OPTICAL DISK FILE SERVER."

SO BORING, FALLING ASLEEP...

Panel 8:

WHUMP

Panel 9: I DON'T KNOW HOW SHE DIED. I WAS TELLING HER ABOUT AN OPTICAL...

ZZZZZZ

66

CAN YOU HELP ME?

NO, I'M AFRAID I CAN'T.

YOU SEE, I GET PAID THE SAME LOW HOURLY WAGE WHETHER YOU BUY THAT SHIRT OR NOT. AND AFTER YEARS IN THIS BUSINESS I'VE LEARNED TO DESPISE THE GENERAL PUBLIC.

PLEASE... I HAVE EXACT CHANGE.

I HAVE NO WAY OF KNOWING IF THAT'S TRUE.

EXCUSE ME. DO YOU HAVE ANY PANTS THAT AREN'T A TWELVE-INCH WAIST AND FIFTY INCHES LONG?

I ASK BECAUSE THERE ARE NO HUMAN BEINGS WHO COULD WEAR THESE PANTS, AND ONE OF THE SECRETS OF RETAIL SUCCESS IS TO STOCK MERCHANDISE THAT SOMEBODY MIGHT WANT.

THEN PEOPLE WOULD SHOP HERE AND ACTUALLY BUY THINGS.

WOW, THAT'S WAY HARDER THAN WHAT WE DO.

IT WAS ANOTHER HIDEOUS SHOPPING EXPERIENCE, BUT I FOUND EXACTLY THE PANTS I WANT.

I'M SORRY...

THIS CARD WAS REPORTED STOLEN. THE REAL OWNER WAS STRANGLED WITH HIS OWN PANTS JUST MINUTES AGO ON AISLE SIX...

THAT WOULD EXPLAIN WHY THESE WERE ON THE FLOOR BY THE CHALK OUTLINE.

DILBERT, I WANT YOU TO HELP SUSAN PUT THE DEPARTMENT BUDGET TOGETHER.

BUDGET?!

NO, PLEASE! I'LL BE BRANDED FOR LIFE. THE OTHER ENGINEERS WILL SPIT ON ME.

DARN, HIS GUARD IS UP.

I'LL HAVE TO WEAR A RAINCOAT TO WORK!

5-10

DILBERT IS ASSIGNED TO PREPARE THE BUDGET.

YOU'LL HAVE TO LEARN OUR BUDGET SYSTEM.

IT WAS DEVELOPED 400 YEARS AGO BY A CRAZED MONK WHO SEALED HIM-SELF IN A WINE CASK.

5-11

UNFORTUNATELY, WE STILL HAVE HIM.

HEY, I'VE GOT ANOTHER IDEA.

THE OTHER ENGINEERS SHUN ME BECAUSE I'M ASSIGNED TO WORK ON THE BUDGET.

SHUN

5-12

THEY KNOW I COULD POUNCE ANY MOMENT AND ASK INANE HYPOTHETICAL BUDGET QUESTIONS.

SHUN

WHAT IF YOU ONLY HAD HALF AS MUCH ELECTRICITY NEXT YEAR?

TOO LATE. I SHUNNED YOU.

HEY, "DIL-BUTT," I HEAR THEY GOT YOU DOING BUDGET WORK NOW.

HA HA! IT MUST BE REALLY EXCITING WORK. I MEAN, GOSH, MAKING ALL THOSE NUMBERS ADD UP.

5-13

HA HA! I'M GLAD I HAVE A REAL JOB!

NOT ANY-MORE.

CLICK

HOW CAN I BE SURE I'M A RAT?

WHAT IF I'M REALLY SOMETHING ELSE — LIKE A POTATO — AND I JUST THINK I'M A RAT?

5-14

I THINK, THEREFORE I'M A YAM.

IT WOULD EXPLAIN A LOT.

I NEVER LEARNED TO READ, BUT IT DIDN'T MATTER BECAUSE I WAS A GREAT ATHLETE.

5-15

THEN CAME THE MULTI-MILLION DOLLAR CONTRACT, WHICH I SPENT ON DRUGS. EVENTUALLY I WAS BANNED FROM SPORTS. I QUIT DRUGS BECAUSE I COULDN'T AFFORD IT.

NOW I'M A MOTIVA-TIONAL SPEAKER.

HAVE YOU MOTI-VATED ANYBODY TO BECOME ILLITERATE YET?

MY "DEFANTALATOR" INVENTION CAN ELIMINATE THE UNPRODUCTIVE AND NAUGHTY THOUGHTS OF YOUR MALE EMPLOYEES.

WE SUCCEEDED IN GETTING MEN TO STOP ACTING LIKE MEN, BUT IT WASN'T ENOUGH. MEN MUST STOP THINKING LIKE MEN TOO.

5-27

HEY! CUT IT OUT!

HMM... A LITTLE MAKE-UP AND A NEW HAIR-DO...

© 1993 United Feature Syndicate, Inc.

THERE'S ANOTHER UNPRODUCTIVE MAN, DAYDREAMING ABOUT ATTRACTIVE WOMEN.

A SHORT BURST FROM MY "DE-FANTALATOR" SHOULD SET HIM STRAIGHT.

WUSSS

5-28

HEY! I THINK I'M STARTING TO LIKE FIGURE SKATING!

© 1993 United Feature Syndicate, Inc.

OUR SCHOOL SYSTEM IS A COMPLETE FAILURE, DOGBERT.

WHY'S THAT?

5-29

THE SCHOOLS SHOULD BE PREPARING THESE KIDS TO BE SCIENTISTS AND ENGINEERS. THAT'S THE ONLY WAY OUR ECONOMY WILL PROSPER.

© 1993 United Feature Syndicate, Inc.

INSTEAD, WE'LL BE A NATION OF MAIDS AND JANITORS.

YEAH, BUT THINK HOW CLEAN IT WILL BE.

I CAN'T WAIT TO GROW UP AND GET OUT OF SCHOOL.

ACTUALLY, NORIKO, YOUR GENERATION WILL HAVE TO TAKE CLASSES AND WORK FULL-TIME YOUR WHOLE LIVES ... ASSUMING ANY JOBS EXIST.

5-31

BUT ON THE PLUS SIDE, TELEVISION WILL HAVE A THOUSAND CHANNELS.

THAT'S IT; SOMEBODY'S GOT SOME EXPLAINING TO DO!

WHO THE HECK IS RUNNING THIS PLANET??! IT'S A TOTAL DISASTER!!

THE ENVIRONMENT IS A MESS! CRIME AND POVERTY EVERYWHERE!! WHO'S RESPONSIBLE?!!

ADULTS, LIKE HIM.

6-1

HI, NORIKO. IS SOMETHING WRONG?

DUHHH!

YOU ADULTS HAVE TOTALLY MESSED UP THE PLANET!! WHERE'S THE ACCOUNTABILITY??!

YOU KNOW OUR IMPLIED SOCIAL CONTRACT! YOU TAKE CARE OF THE KIDS, THEN WE TAKE CARE OF YOU WHEN YOU'RE OLD. THAT'S HOW IT'S SUPPOSED TO WORK.

WELL, I ...

THE DEAL IS OFF!!

6-2

YOU ADULTS ARE RUINING THE PLANET FOR MY GENERATION.

WE KIDS HAVE NO POWER NOW, BUT I'M TAKING NAMES. WHEN WE TAKE POWER WE'LL SHIP YOU ALL TO A PENAL COLONY ON MARS.

6-3

THERE'S NO OXYGEN ON MARS.

OH, *NOW* YOU LEARN TO PLAN AHEAD.

NORIKO, I'D LIKE YOU TO MEET BOB THE DINOSAUR.

HI

HI

I THOUGHT DINOSAURS WERE ALL EXTINCT.

NO, THEY WERE JUST HIDING. WE FOUND BOB BEHIND THE COUCH.

6-4

I WISH WE HAD ONE AT OUR HOUSE.

LOOK IN YOUR CREDENZA. THE BELMONTS LIVE IN THE "KRAZY GLUE" DRAWER.

TAKE BOB WITH YOU, NORIKO. YOU'LL NEED HELP SAVING THE PLANET FOR YOUR GENERATION.

6-5

I HAVE A BLACK BELT IN KARATE. WHAT SKILLS DO YOU BRING TO THE PARTY?

WEDGIES, MOSTLY.

IT'S NOT AS MENACING AS KARATE, BUT YOU HAVE TO LOVE THE EXPRESSIONS ON THEIR FACES.

TURN HIM THIS WAY.

IT'S TIME FOR YOUR ANNUAL PERFORMANCE REVIEW.

THE PROCESS IS THE SAME AS USUAL.

MAKE YOUR ACCOMPLISHMENTS FIT THE TRENDY CATEGORIES ON THIS FORM.

"1. ESTIMATE THE CASH VALUE OF THE EMPOWERMENT YOU DISPLAYED THIS YEAR. CITE EXAMPLES."

TRY TO MAKE YOUR ACCOMPLISHMENTS MATCH THE RAISE I'VE ALREADY DECIDED FOR YOU.

WHY DON'T YOU JUST TELL ME WHAT YOU'VE DECIDED?

WHAT -- AND RUIN THE MOTIVATIONAL VALUE OF THE PROCESS ??

HOW DID I GET STUCK WITH ALL THE CYNICAL EMPLOYEES ?

S. Adams

© 1993 United Feature Syndicate, Inc.

6-6

81

STOP RIGHT THERE, MISTER ADULT! YOU'VE GOT SOME EXPLAINING TO DO TO MY GENERATION!

IT'S QUITE SIMPLE, REALLY. CHILDREN HAVE NO POLITICAL POWER. SO WE ADULTS CAN PLUNDER THE PLANET, RUN UP HUGE DEBTS, THEN DIE FAT AND HAPPY!

I'VE NEVER SEEN ANYBODY LIFTED BY HIS BRIEFS AND SPUN IN THE AIR LIKE THAT.

THAT'S MY "TWIRLING WEDGIE."

THIS IS DOGBERT, WITH A BROADCAST E-MAIL MESSAGE TO ALL COMPUTER GEEKS...

I DECLARE MYSELF TO BE YOUR LEADER. AND I NAME MY EMPIRE THE "VIRTUAL ELECTRONIC NATION OF DOGBERT," VENOD FOR SHORT.

I ASSUME YOU'LL BE EXPLOITING THE SIMPLE PEOPLE OF VENOD FOR PERSONAL GAIN.

YEAH, IT'S A LEADERSHIP TRADITION.

NOW THAT YOU'VE UNITED THE ELECTRONIC MAIL USERS OF THE WORLD, WHAT ARE YOU GOING TO DO?

I'LL POLL THEM ABOUT THEIR NEEDS, THEN USE THEIR COLLECTIVE POLITICAL AND ECONOMIC POWER TO GET THEM WHATEVER THE MAJORITY WANTS.

COULDN'T YOU EASILY RIG THE VOTE TO SUPPORT YOUR OWN SELFISH AMBITIONS?

I LOVE THE DEMOCRATIC SYSTEM.

I AM DOGBERT, LEADER OF VENOD — A HUGE COLLECTIVE OF NERDS. WE DEMAND TWENTY PERCENT DISCOUNTS ON ALL OF YOUR PRODUCTS.

IF YOU REFUSE, I WILL SEND A WIRELESS E-MAIL MESSAGE THAT INSTRUCTS ONE MILLION NERDS TO STOP BUYING YOUR PRODUCTS.

YOU'RE KIDDING, RIGHT?

THERE — I JUST SENT THEM YOUR DAUGHTER'S PHONE NUMBER.

AREN'T YOU AFRAID THAT IF YOU CONTINUE AS LEADER OF THE NERDS, YOU WILL BECOME A NERD YOURSELF.

NO, BECAUSE YOU CAN'T BECOME A NERD UNLESS YOU HAVE A GENETIC PREDISPOSITION TOWARD IT.

LOOK! I ADDED AN EMERGENCY BACKUP POCKET!

SEE? YOU CAN'T LEARN THAT STUFF IN COMPUTER CLASS.

THERE... I'VE ORGANIZED ALL OF MY TASKS INTO "A," "B" AND "C" PRIORITIES.

THE "A" PRIORITIES AREN'T EVEN WORTH DOING. AND THE "B" PRIORITY STUFF WOULD PROBABLY GET ME IN TROUBLE.

ARE YOU DONE WITH THE STAPLER OIL?

THANK GOODNESS FOR "C" PRIORITIES.

I TOOK A CRACK AT WRITING A "MISSION STATEMENT" FOR OUR GROUP.

"WE ENHANCE STOCKHOLDER VALUE THROUGH STRATEGIC BUSINESS INITIATIVES BY EMPOWERED EMPLOYEES WORKING IN NEW TEAM PARADIGMS."

DO YOU EVER JUST MARVEL AT THE FACT WE GET PAID TO DO THIS?

DID ANYBODY BRING DONUTS?

I GOT A BROCHURE FOR "DOGBERT'S SEMINAR ON MANAGEMENT ZOMBIES." I THINK YOU SHOULD GO.

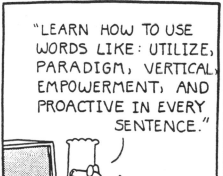

"LEARN HOW TO USE WORDS LIKE: UTILIZE, PARADIGM, VERTICAL EMPOWERMENT, AND PROACTIVE IN EVERY SENTENCE."

I'M NOT SURE I WANT TO TALK LIKE THAT.

COME... JOIN US... DON'T BE AFRAID...

MANY OF YOU COME TO MY MANAGEMENT SEMINAR AS OPTIMISTIC, CREATIVE, CLEAR-SPEAKING INDIVIDUALS.

BUT WITH HARD WORK, YOU CAN BECOME JARGON-SPEWING CORPORATE ZOMBIES, LIKE CARL HERE.

I WANT TO DIALOGUE WITH YOU ABOUT UTILIZING RESOURCES.

GOOD BOY! HERE'S A DONUT.

Panel 1:

DOGBERT'S SEMINAR ON MANAGEMENT ZOMBIES

THE SUCCESSFUL ZOMBIE KNOWS HOW TO SQUASH THE CREATIVITY OF CO-WORKERS.

Panel 2:

WHEN YOU HEAR A NEW IDEA, ADOPT A FACIAL EXPRESSION WHICH CONVEYS BOTH FEAR AND AN UTTER LACK OF COMPREHENSION.

6-17

Panel 3:

THOSE OF YOU WHO WORK IN MARKETING ONLY NEED TO ADD THE FEAR PART.

WHY IS THAT?

Panel 4:

DOGBERT'S SEMINAR ON MANAGEMENT ZOMBIES

TO BE A ZOMBIE YOU MUST DRINK THE ZOMBIE ELIXIR.

Panel 5:

THE ZOMBIE ELIXIR WILL REMOVE ANY DISTRACTING THOUGHTS OF SLEEP OR FAMILY LIFE.

Panel 6:

IT LOOKS LIKE COFFEE.

YOU HAVE TO ADD ONE SCOOP OF ZOMBIE SUGAR.

6-18

Panel 7:

DOGBERT'S SEMINAR ON MANAGEMENT ZOMBIES

AS A ZOMBIE, YOU MUST SPEAK IN EMPTY GENERAL-ITIES.

Panel 8:

YOUR BUSINESS PLAN MIGHT SAY "WE STRIVE TO UTILIZE A VARIETY OF TECHNIQUES TO ACCOMPLISH A BROAD SPECTRUM OF RESULTS TOWARD THE BOTTOM LINE."

6-19

Panel 9:

HEY! MY SKIN IS GETTING CLAMMY AND I HAVE THE URGE TO CALL A MEETING!

ME TOO!

GOOD... GOOD...

As you know, all projects are assigned acronyms. Unfortunately, all the good ones have been used.

Any new project will have to use an acronym from this short list of somewhat less desirable choices.

Panel 1:
YESTERDAY WE RAN OUT OF ACRONYMS. TODAY WE USED OUR LAST ACCOUNTING CODE. WE'RE IN BIG TROUBLE.

Panel 2:
WHY DON'T WE JUST REPROGRAM THE COMPUTERS TO ACCEPT LONGER CODES?

A PROJECT LIKE THAT WOULD NEED AN ACRONYM AND AN ACCOUNTING CODE.

Panel 3:
WHY NOT REUSE A CODE FROM A PROJECT THAT'S COMPLETE?

ODDLY ENOUGH, WE'VE NEVER COMPLETED A PROJECT.

Panel 4:
I AM ALICE THE COMPULSIVE GRABBER.

Panel 5:
WHEN I SEE THINGS THAT ARE NOT RIGHT I MUST GRAB THEM.

Panel 6:
IN AN HOUR OR SO I MAY HAVE TO ASK YOU TO STOP THAT.

Panel 7:

Panel 8:
SQUEEZE SQUEEZE SQUEEZE

Panel 9:
IN RETROSPECT, THAT WAS EXACTLY THE KIND OF TEMPTATION I SHOULD JUST IGNORE.

MY PATENT WILL MAKE FIFTY MILLION DOLLARS FOR THE COMPANY, SO I THOUGHT MAYBE YOU COULD AFFORD TO GIVE ME A RAISE.

UNFORTUNATELY, THE PROFIT BUCKET IS NOT CONNECTED TO THE BUDGET BUCKET, SO THERE'S NO MONEY FOR A RAISE.

I THINK SOME RECOGNITION OF A JOB WELL-DONE IS APPROPRIATE HERE.

THANKS. IT WAS ONE OF MY BETTER EXCUSES.

DOGBERT, TELL ME IF YOU THINK MY ILLUSTRATION FOR TOMORROW'S PRESENTATION IS CLEAR.

AH, YES. YOU'RE SAYING THE FACE OF ELVIS WILL APPEAR ON A CREDENZA AFTER BEING STRUCK BY LIGHTNING.

THAT'S SUPPOSED TO BE A VIDEO TELECONFERENCE.

I DIDN'T KNOW YOU COULD DO THAT WITH A CREDENZA.

PLEASE EXCUSE THE ARTWORK IN THIS NEXT DIAGRAM.

WHAT'S THAT? IT LOOKS LIKE ELVIS' FACE ON A CREDENZA! HA HA HA! OR IS IT A RORSCHACH TEST??! HA HA HA!!

AND IN CONCLUSION, I HATE YOU ALL.

LET'S START WITH A BRAINSTORMING EXERCISE. ALICE, YOU GO FIRST.

I IMAGINE MYSELF NOT SURROUNDED BY DULL, UNATTRACTIVE, AND LARGELY CLUELESS MEN.

I THINK SHE JUST INSULTED YOU GUYS.

MMMM...

I'VE IDENTIFIED THE BRAIN CHEMICAL THAT CONTROLS HAPPINESS.

AND I FOUND THE EXACT MIX OF FRUIT AND VEGETABLE JUICES THAT STIMULATE ITS PRODUCTION.

DO YOU REALIZE WHAT THIS MEANS?

YEAH. FRUITS AND VEGETABLES WILL BE BANNED BY THE GOVERNMENT.

WE'RE THE GOVERNMENT. WE CAME TO CONFISCATE YOUR SO-CALLED "HAPPINESS DRUG."

IT'S NOT A DRUG! IT'S JUST A MIXTURE OF FRUITS AND VEGETABLES THAT MAKES YOU FEEL HAPPY! YOU CAN'T OUTLAW GOOD NUTRITION!

HMM... I GUESS THAT WOULDN'T MAKE SENSE, WOULD IT?

IGNORE HIM. HE'S A NEW GUY.

ERASE ALL THE FORMULAS FOR MAKING YOUR "HAPPINESS POTION" AND WE WON'T JAIL YOU.

OKAY, OKAY...

YOU CITIZENS ONLY HAVE THE RIGHT TO PURSUE HAPPINESS — YOU'RE NOT ALLOWED TO BE HAPPY.

CITIZENS NEED DISCOMFORT IN ORDER TO BE PRODUCTIVE AND FULFILLED.

WEDGIE

THEN YOU'LL LOVE THIS...

WHAT ARE YOU MAKING?

COMMEMORATIVE COLLECTIBLE PLATES.

ONE OF THE MYSTERIES OF LIFE IS THAT YOU CAN PUT ANY PICTURE ON A PLATE AND HORDES OF MORONS WILL WANT TO OWN IT.

WOW! AN ACORN! AND IT'S ON A PLATE!

WHAT'S IT LIKE TO BE A MEMBER OF A HORDE?

YOU ALREADY OWN THE "ACORN SERIES" OF DOGBERT'S COMMEMORATIVE PLATES...

FOR A LIMITED TIME YOU MAY ALSO PURCHASE MY NEW ISSUE. THE "FRENCH GUY WITH A HAT" SERIES.

MY ACORN PLATES ARE MISSING.

TOMORROW I'LL INTRODUCE MY NEW SERIES: "RUSSIAN WITH FRENCH HAT."

I THOUGHT OF ANOTHER WAY TO PROFIT FROM THE IGNORANCE OF HUMANS.

7-12

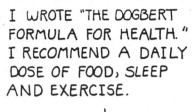

I WROTE "THE DOGBERT FORMULA FOR HEALTH." I RECOMMEND A DAILY DOSE OF FOOD, SLEEP AND EXERCISE.

AND FOR ONLY $19.95 YOU CAN BUY THE PATENTED "DOGBERT JOGGEROBIC CARPET PATCH" TO HELP YOU RUN IN PLACE.

ARE YOU TIRED OF FAD DIETS AND FAD EXERCISE DEVICES?

YES I AM!

7-13

THEN BUY MY BOOK AND GET THE REVOLUTIONARY JOGGEROBIC CARPET PATCH FOR ONLY $19.95 PLUS SHIPPING AND HANDLING.

TO PROVE IT WORKS, WE PHOTOGRAPHED AN ACTUAL ATHLETE.

PICTURES DON'T LIE!

IT LOOKS LIKE SALES OF THE "DOGBERT JOGGEROBIC CARPET PATCH" ARE BRISK.

YEAH, AND I'M LOOKING TO EXPAND.

7-14

RATBERT IS BUSY RESEARCHING NEW PRODUCT CONCEPTS FOR THE CARPET PATCH.

"CARPET CLUB FOR MEN."

I THINK I'VE HIT UPON A BRILLIANT NEW DIRECTION FOR EXPANDING OUR PRODUCT LINE.

I CALL THEM "CARPET PATCH KIDS." EACH ONE IS MADE FROM CARPET AND HAS ITS OWN NAME!

DON'T FEEL BAD, RAQUEL. I DON'T THINK HE MEANT IT AS A PERSONAL ATTACK.

7-15

OUR NEWEST FAD POLICY IS TO HAVE SUBORDINATES APPRAISE THEIR BOSS'S JOB PERFORMANCE.

I GIVE YOU A "D MINUS."

DID I MENTION RETRIBUTION?

CAREFUL, SIR; YOU'RE HANGING BY A THREAD.

7-16

SOMETIMES I THINK I'M NOT REACHING MY FULL POTENTIAL AS A RAT.

YOU'RE RIGHT. IN THE MIDDLE AGES, DISEASE-CARRYING RATS WIPED OUT HALF OF THE HUMAN POPULATION OF EUROPE.

I THINK I'VE GOT A LITTLE TEMPERATURE. FEEL MY FOREHEAD.

FACE IT, YOUR GLORY DAYS ARE PAST.

7-17

YOUR NEW PROJECT WILL HAVE NO BUDGET AND NO MANAGEMENT SUPPORT. EXPECT TO SPEND MOST OF YOUR TIME GIVING STATUS REPORTS.

OH NO! THE LIFE FORCE HAS BEEN DRAINED OUT OF ME! I'M BECOMING A DAMP RAG!?!

7-19

THAT'S AMAZING.

IT'S NOTHING. I DID EIGHTEEN AT ONCE AT THE EMPLOYEE EMPOWERMENT BRUNCH.

© 1993 United Feature Syndicate, Inc.

I'LL BE REPRESENTING YOU CORPORATE EMPLOYEES IN A CLASS ACTION SUIT. YOUR COMPANY HAS SUCKED THE LIFE FORCE OUT OF YOU AND TURNED YOU INTO LITTLE RAGS.

MY FEE WILL BE ON A CONTINGENCY BASIS. THAT MEANS I GET THE ENTIRE SETTLEMENT PLUS I'LL USE YOU TO WAX MY BMW.

7-20

I'VE FOUND THE PERFECT CLIENTS.

SOUNDS FAIR.

DON'T MAKE WAVES.

© 1993 United Feature Syndicate, Inc.

I'M FROM THE LAW FIRM OF DOGBERT, DOGBERT AND DOGBERT. I'M SUING YOU FOR DRAINING THE LIFE FORCE OUT OF YOUR EMPLOYEES.

AFTER BEING DRAINED OF LIFE, EMPLOYEES ARE FORCED TO LEAVE THE COMPANY. THE LUCKY ONES GET JOBS AS RAGS FOR A CAR WASH, LIKE JOEY PISHKIN HERE.

© 1993 United Feature Syndicate, Inc.

HONK HONK

WHAT JOEY? THAT'S MARGE FROM ACCOUNTING???

7-21

IF YOU DO NOT DROP YOUR CLASS ACTION SUIT, THEN YOU'LL HAVE TO FACE ME IN COURT.

AND I'VE NEVER LOST A CASE.

THEN HOW DO YOU KNOW YOU WOULDN'T ENJOY IT.

WELL... I JUST WOULDN'T.

GOOD ARGUMENT.

FOR MY FIRST WITNESS, I CALL THE DEFENDANT'S ATTORNEY.

IS IT TRUE THAT YOU'RE WEARING WOMEN'S LINGERIE RIGHT NOW?

NO!

IS THIS RELEVANT TO YOUR CASE?

I WONDER WHY YOU'RE SO TOUCHY ABOUT THIS SUBJECT.

BEFORE YOU DECIDE WHO WINS THIS CIVIL SUIT, REMEMBER THIS...

I CAN'T LEGALLY OFFER YOU LARGE CASH KICK-BACKS FOR DECIDING IN MY FAVOR. BUT PLEASE TAKE A MOMENT TO COMPLETE A SELF-ADDRESSED STAMPED ENVELOPE.

WHAT ARE YOU DOING?

I'M TRYING TO ESTABLISH "REASONABLE DOUBT."

THE JURY HAS REACHED A DECISION IN THE CASE OF "DOGBERT VS. A BIG CORPORATION."

WE AWARD DOGBERT FIFTY MILLION DOLLARS BECAUSE WE HATE BIG COMPANIES AND WE LIKE LITTLE DOGS WITH GLASSES.

I HATE MY LIFE.

AND WE AWARD A MAYTAG DRYER TO JUROR MINDY FOR BEING "BEST DRESSED."

DOES IT BOTHER YOU THAT I WON FIFTY MILLION DOLLARS IN MY LAWSUIT, WHEREAS YOU STILL TOIL TO REMAIN MIDDLE CLASS?

DOES IT BOTHER YOU TO KNOW THAT I COULD BUY YOU AND SELL YOU... HOW MANY TIMES?

834 TIMES.

HEY, IT'S GONE UP SINCE LUNCH!

...SO I THOUGHT YOU MIGHT USE SOME OF YOUR NEWLY WON MILLIONS TO FUND MY "BIOWORLD" SCIENCE EXPERIMENT.

IT'S A COMPLETE ECOLOGY ENCLOSED IN AN AIRTIGHT DOME. THE SURVIVAL OF THE VOLUNTEERS WOULD DEPEND ON MY FORESIGHT AND ENGINEERING SKILLS.

GEE, I THOUGHT IT WOULD BE HARDER TO TALK YOU INTO IT.

I GET TO PICK THE VOLUNTEERS MYSELF.

I'VE COMPLETED THE DESIGN FOR BIOWORLD. HAVE YOU SELECTED THE VOLUNTEERS?

YES.

BIOWORLD

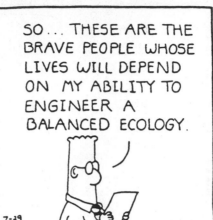

SO... THESE ARE THE BRAVE PEOPLE WHOSE LIVES WILL DEPEND ON MY ABILITY TO ENGINEER A BALANCED ECOLOGY.

7-29

SEVEN CAR SALESMEN PLUS RATBERT...

COINCIDENCE.

THE BIOWORLD DOME IS NOW SEALED. YOU MUST LIVE OFF ITS RESOURCES FOR TWO YEARS.

THE EDIBLE PLANTS WERE DELIVERED JUST BEFORE THE DOME WAS SEALED. THEY ARE THE KEY TO YOUR SURVIVAL.

7-30

CAN SOMEBODY OPEN THE DELIVERY DOOR? I'VE GOT SOME PLANTS OUTSIDE.

"DAY ONE OF THE BIOWORLD EXPERIMENT IS OFF TO A ROCKY START."

7-31

"THE VOLUNTEERS HAVE NO EDIBLE PLANTS AND THE OXYGEN LEVEL IS DROPPING."

LET US OUT

HELP

FORTUNATELY, MOST OF THE VOLUNTEERS ARE EX-CAR SALESPEOPLE, SO WE REMAIN EMOTIONALLY UNINVOLVED.

LOOK HOW THEY SPELLED "OXYGEN."

WITH OXYGEN AND FOOD NEARLY DEPLETED, THE BIOWORLD VOLUNTEERS BECOME PHILOSOPHICAL.

8-2

SOME OF THE VOLUNTEERS THINK THAT BECAUSE THEY'RE CAR SALESPEOPLE YOU DON'T VALUE THEIR LIVES...

IF THAT WERE TRUE, HOW CAN YOU EXPLAIN THAT WE PUT YOU IN THERE TOO?

THAT'S WHAT I SAID, BUT IT DIDN'T SEEM TO CHEER THEM UP.

© 1993 United Feature Syndicate, Inc.

PLEASE... END THE BIOWORLD EXPERIMENT. WE'RE OUT OF FOOD. AIR IS ALMOST GONE

WE PRAY THERE WAS NO SADISTIC INTENT WHEN YOU CHOSE ONLY CAR SALESPEOPLE FOR THE EXPERIMENT... PLEASE... AT LEAST LET SOME AIR IN...

8-3

GEE, I REALLY WANT TO HELP. I'LL GO TRY TO CONVINCE MY BOSS TO SEE IT YOUR WAY.

HEY! I'M A "SATURN" DEALER — I'M DIFFERENT!

© 1993 United Feature Syndicate, Inc.

IT USED TO BOTHER ME THAT THE AIR WAS GETTING POLLUTED AND UNBREATHABLE.

NEWS

S. Adams

BUT I REALIZED THAT RATS ARE HARDIER THAN HUMANS — SO WE'LL GET ALL YOUR STUFF AFTER YOU WHEEZE YOUR LAST BREATH!

8-4

© 1993 United Feature Syndicate, Inc.

I THINK I'LL GO FOR A WALK.

HEY! WHY NOT DRIVE?

YOU KNOW, AS A RAT I'M FAR MORE LIKELY TO SURVIVE A MAJOR ENVIRONMENTAL CALAMITY.

AND THERE'S NO SHORTAGE OF POTENTIAL DISASTERS — YOU'VE GOT GLOBAL WARMING, OZONE DEPLETION, AIR POLLUTION...

8-5

CAN I TRY ON ONE OF YOUR SHIRTS?

© 1993 United Feature Syndicate, Inc.

I'D MISS YOU IF THE HUMAN RACE DIED FROM POLLUTION BUT RATS LIVED ON.

SO I'M DEDICATING MY LIFE TO LEARNING THE SCIENCE OF PRESERVING HUMAN-KIND.

8-6

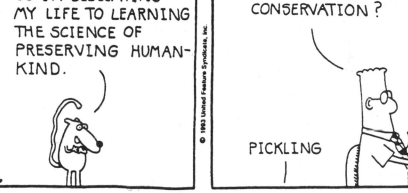

CONSERVATION?

PICKLING

© 1993 United Feature Syndicate, Inc.

THIS SHOW IS GARBAGE. I WILL ESCHEW IT.

CLICK

S. Adams

THAT EXPLAINS YOUR BREATH.

YOU'RE IN YOUR OWN LITTLE WORLD, AREN'T YOU?

8-7

Panel 1: I'VE GOT TO CUT STAFF IN ENGINEERING. I'M TRYING TO DETERMINE WHICH ONE OF YOU IS MORE VALUABLE TO KEEP.

Panel 2: I'VE BEEN HEARING GOOD THINGS ABOUT ZIMBU THE MONKEY. WHICH ONE OF YOU IS ZIMBU THE MONKEY?

Panel 3: THIS IS NOT THE PROUDEST MOMENT OF MY PROFESSIONAL CAREER.

Panel 4: IT'S GOING TO BE TOUGH DECIDING WHICH OF YOU TO LAY OFF.

Panel 5: I WANT TO KEEP THE EMPLOYEE WHO PROJECTS THE MOST PROFESSIONAL IMAGE.

Panel 6: THIS SHOULD MAKE HIM LOOK PRETTY STUPID.

Panel 7: I CAN'T DECIDE WHICH ONE OF YOU TO LAY OFF, SO I'VE DECIDED TO HAVE A CONTEST.

Panel 8: THE FIRST EVENT IS THE "STAPLE CHASE."

Panel 9: ROUND ONE: ZIMBU.

I THINK I WINGED HIM.

DILBERT AND ZIMBU COMPETE FOR ONE JOB.

THIS NEXT EVENT TESTS YOUR HUMOR AND CREATIVITY.

THE OBJECTIVE IS TO SEE HOW MUCH FUN YOU CAN HAVE IN THE BARREL. WHO WANTS TO GO FIRST?

8-12

THIS IS NO FAIR. ZIMBU IS A MONKEY. HE HAS AN ADVANTAGE.

ACTUALLY, THIS IS A TEST OF YOUR GULLIBILITY.

© 1993 United Feature Syndicate, Inc.

AFTER COMPARING THE TWO OF YOU, I'VE DECIDED TO KEEP DILBERT FOR THE LAST ENGINEERING JOB.

8-13

YES! I WIN, YOU LITTLE BANANA-EATING-FLEA-HOTEL! HA HA HA HA!!!

© 1993 United Feature Syndicate, Inc.

I'M PUTTING ZIMBU ON THE MANAGEMENT FAST-TRACK.

BAD TIME FOR THE VICTORY JIG.

© 1993 United Feature Syndicate, Inc.

DOES ANYBODY HAVE ANY QUESTIONS ABOUT OUR PLAN? ASK ME ANYTHING — THERE ARE NO "STUPID" QUESTIONS.

IF YOU CROSSED THE INTERNATIONAL DATE LINE ON YOUR BIRTHDAY, WOULD YOU STILL GET PRESENTS?

8-14

© 1993 United Feature Syndicate, Inc.

OH GREAT... THERE ARE STUPID QUESTIONS AND I DON'T KNOW THE ANSWERS.

I'M TOLD BY A RELIABLE SOURCE THAT OUR SENIOR VICE PRESIDENT MADE A SOUND LIKE "YURP" AT LUNCH.

WHAT DOES IT MEAN? DOES IT SIGNAL A NEW SET OF PRIORITIES? WE MUST DEMONSTRATE OUR COMMITMENT TO THIS VISION.

WHAT WAS THE CONTEXT OF THIS VISION?

ALL WE KNOW IS HE WAS EATING A BURRITO.

I AM DOGBERT THE PSYCHIC BUSINESS CONSULTANT. I CAN READ MINDS.

IF YOU CAN READ MINDS, WHAT'S MY FAVORITE COLOR?

YOUR FAVORITE COLOR IS PUCE, BUT YOU ARE MISTAKENLY THINKING OF A PRIMARY COLOR BECAUSE YOU DON'T KNOW WHAT PUCE IS.

WHOA... I JUST GOT A SHIVER

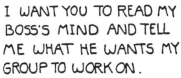

I WANT YOU TO READ MY BOSS'S MIND AND TELL ME WHAT HE WANTS MY GROUP TO WORK ON.

WHY DON'T YOU JUST ASK HIM?

ASK HIM?? I CAN'T DO THAT. HIS CALENDAR IS BOOKED FOR MONTHS. AND I NEVER UNDERSTAND WHAT HE SAYS ANYWAY.

HE THINKS YOU'RE AN IDIOT, BUT IT'S EASIER TO PAY YOU THAN TO FIRE YOU.

WHEW! JOB SECURITY.

I'M SENDING YOU TO OUR PLANT IN ELBONIA. I WANT YOU TO TEACH THEM "QUALITY."

I SELECTED YOU BECAUSE YOU'VE BEEN THERE AND YOU KNOW THEIR LANGUAGE.

THEY SPEAK ENGLISH.

OH. THEN I GUESS IT'S BECAUSE I HATE YOU.

I'LL GO WITH YOU ON YOUR TRIP TO ELBONIA. I CAN BE YOUR BODYGUARD!

IT'S NOT A GOOD PLACE FOR A RAT. THE MUD IS QUITE...

YOU THINK I'M NOT TOUGH ENOUGH? I'LL SHOW YOU!!

ELBONIA

AND THAT'S YOUR BODY-GUARD?

I DON'T LIKE THE TONE OF YOUR VOICE.

ELBONIA

I'VE BEEN SENT TO TEACH YOU "TOTAL QUALITY MANAGE-MENT."

IN THE OLD DAYS, QUALITY WAS JUST AN EMPTY WORD MEANING "GOOD."

QUALITY EQUALS GOOD (1950)

EVENTUALLY IT EVOLVED INTO A COMPLICATED METHOD FOR TRANS-FERRING YOUR MONEY TO BUSINESS CONSULTANTS.

DILBERT TEACHES ELBONIA "TOTAL QUALITY" METHODS.

YOU START BY IDENTIFYING PROBLEM AREAS.

HMM... SOMETIMES OUR MITTENS GET STUCK TO OUR NOSES AND WE CAN'T BREATHE.

SNIFF

YORGI! TRY TO BREATHE WITH YOUR MOUTH!

MMM! MMM!

PEOPLE! LET'S TALK METRICS, PLEASE!

© 1993 United Feature Syndicate, Inc.

8-26

DILBERT TEACHES "QUALITY" MANAGEMENT IN ELBONIA

THE FISHBONE DIAGRAM HELPS IDENTIFY THE ROOT CAUSE OF PROB-LEMS.

IN YOUR CASE, THE ROOT PROBLEM SEEMS TO BE THAT YOU'RE A NATION OF IMBECILES...

© 1993 United Feature Syndicate, Inc.

TRUE, BUT YOU'RE THE ONE WHO HAD TO DRAW A DEAD FISH TO FIGURE IT OUT.

YOU'RE IN THE CLUB! HERE'S YOUR HAT.

8-27

THANK YOU FOR TEACH-ING US "QUALITY" TECHNIQUES.

MANUFACTURING DEFECTS ARE DOWN FIFTY PERCENT SINCE WE ALL JOINED "QUALITY TEAMS."

YES!

© 1993 United Feature Syndicate, Inc.

8-28

HOW'S OUR PRODUCTIVITY, YORGI?

DOWN FIFTY PERCENT.

THEY'RE ON TO ME.

S. Adams

I FIGURED THAT YOU WOULD RESPECT ME MORE IF I HAD SOME SORT OF TALENT.

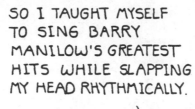

SO I TAUGHT MYSELF TO SING BARRY MANILOW'S GREATEST HITS WHILE SLAPPING MY HEAD RHYTHMICALLY.

A-A-AT THE COPA SLAP OW! COPA CABANA SLAP OW!

I'M ACTUALLY ENJOYING THIS AND IT DEEPLY DISTURBS ME.

WHAT ARE YOU FILMING?

RATBERT GOT HIS OWN CABLE TV CHANNEL.

NOW THAT CABLE TV HAS A THOUSAND CHANNELS THEY'RE DESPERATE FOR ORIGINAL PROGRAMS.

BACK IN THE SIX-HUNDREDS I SAW A RAT SLAPPING HIS HEAD TO A BARRY MANILOW TUNE.

THAT'S WORTH A SECOND LOOK.

THE WATER FOR MY SPAGHETTI SHOULD BE BOILING BY NOW.

OOPS! YOU CAUGHT ME. I USUALLY FINISH HOT TUBBING BEFORE YOU GET BACK.

IT RAISES A BIG QUESTION MARK ABOUT THE CAPERS.

CAPERS?

122

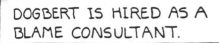

DOGBERT IS HIRED AS A BLAME CONSULTANT.

THE COMPANY'S WOES ARE <u>YOUR</u> FAULT, NOT SENIOR MANAGEMENT'S!

9-16

DO YOU REALIZE HOW MUCH <u>YOU</u> COULD GAIN PERSONALLY BY MAKING THE COMPANY A SUCCESS?

I WOULD GET A NICE PLAQUE IN A PLASTIC FRAME.

YEAH... I WAS HOPING YOU DIDN'T KNOW.

HERE'S MY CONSULTING REPORT ON YOUR COMPANY.

9-17

I HAD NO INSIGHTS SO I BULKED IT UP BY ADDING WITTY ANALOGIES.

"HIS HEAD WAS LIKE A HOLLOW PUTTY BALL ATTACKED BY TWO POINTY DUST BUNNIES."

VIVID, ISN'T IT?

RATBERT, DID YOU KNOW THAT YOUR BRAIN AUTOMATICALLY COORDINATES MILLIONS OF ACTIVITIES EVERY SECOND?

9-18

IMAGINE IF IT GOT JUST A LITTLE BIT CONFUSED — ALL THOSE NEURONS FIRING RANDOMLY...

YOU DON'T ADD MUCH TO A CONVERSATION, BUT YOU'RE EASILY THE BEST LISTENER I'VE EVER MET.

AAAEE!

I BET I'VE GONE TO JAIL MORE THAN THE AVERAGE LAW-ABIDING CITIZEN.

I PLAN TO DEFEND YOU BY PROVING YOUR VICTIM WAS A TEMP WORKER.

IT'S LEGAL TO KILL A TEMP? REALLY??

NOW ALL WE NEED IS A JURY OF YOUR "PEERS."

YES, MY CLIENT DID ACCIDENTALLY SLAY A "TEMP" WORKER... EMPHASIS ON "TEMP."

BUT WHO AMONG US CAN SAY THEY HAVEN'T SLAIN INNOCENT PEOPLE WHEN THE SITUATION CALLED FOR IT?

I CAN.

WELL, GREAT... SO MUCH FOR GETTING A FAIR TRIAL.

ALTHOUGH THE INSANITY DEFENSE DOES NOT APPLY TO MY CLIENT, WE HAVE SOMETHING JUST AS GOOD.

MY CLIENT IS AN "ENGINEER SAVANT." HE UNDERSTANDS TECHNOLOGY BUT NOTHING ELSE.

AS EVIDENCE, I SUBMIT MY CLIENT'S WHITE SOCKS, COMPLETE WITH THE SOCK PROTECTOR AND AUXILIARY WRITING TOOLS.